THE
WHY-TO
OF
SCUBA
DIVING

JIM CROCKETT

AQUA QUEST PUBLICATIONS, INC. ■ NEW YORK

Library of Congress Cataloging-in-Publication Data

Crockett, Jim.
    The why to of scuba diving / by Jim Crockett.
    p.   cm.
    Summary: Explains why so many people love scuba diving and snorkeling, what they can see underwater, and what it takes to get started, including equipment, places to dive, and careers.
    ISBN 1-881652-21-1 (alk. paper)
    1. Scuba diving—Juvenile literature. [1. Scuba diving.] I. Title: Scuba diving. II. Title.
GV838.672.C74 2000
797.2'3—dc21
                   99-057722

Printed in Hong Kong
10 9 8 7 6 5 4 3 2 1

All photographs are by the author unless otherwise noted.

DEDICATION

For

Roberta
Chenoa
Dara
Cordell
Kessel
Adelaide
Devon

Let's go diving!

CONTENTS

Stores and libraries are packed with books telling you *how* to do things, but this book tells you *why*. Why do so many people love scuba diving? What do they get out of it? What do they see down there? Why do they want to go to the trouble to take lessons, get certified, buy special equipment, and travel to waters that might be miserably cold and difficult to see in? And, can anything go wrong?

Why *do* people scuba dive? Let's find out...

WHAT'S IT LIKE DOWN THERE?

The underwater world is an almost magical place. Often, what appear to be plants are actually living animals; what may look like rocks are frequently living coral "villages" of millions of microorganisms. Most of us think of "animals" as the four-legged type, but beneath the water's surface, there are countless *soft corals* and *anemones* that look exactly like what's growing in your backyard. They rise up in branches or clusters, waving in the water currents. Yet, they are actually living creatures that feed by filtering nutrients from the passing water, reproduce, and sometimes move slowly from place to place. Some of them have created ingeneous ways of luring fish within their grasp, then stinging them, dragging the meal to their mouths to digest it.

In addition, when diving you are almost weightless, and most of the sounds you hear are just your own exhaust bubbles. And, usually, it's a world of gray and blue.

Let's get more specific.

Above is a typical underwater scene in the Caribbean Sea. The orange tube sponges in the center have anchored themselves to a coral head. In the background is a large sea fan that gently waves back and forth in the current, absorbing nutrients from the water. To the **left** is a three-inch-high featherduster. It's actually a worm and extends its filters to feed, but when the animal is startled it contracts its arms down into the tube so quickly you almost can't see it happen. On the **right** is a gorgonian soft coral.

Weightlessness

One of the first sensations you notice underwater is the feeling of being weightless, like you are floating in space. Even though you may be wearing a rubber "wet suit," have an air tank on your back and lead weights around your waist, the water's buoyancy pushes you up. Saltwater, for instance, is so buoyant that without adding lead weights, you'll never be able to get below the surface more than a foot or two.

Yet, even with all the weight and equipment, if you prepare it correctly you'll be as light as air once you get underwater. The goal is to be neutrally buoyant, which means weighting yourself just enough to stay steady and level under the surface—you'll neither rise to the surface nor sink to the bottom. To prepare your equipment correctly, you need to know your weight and that of some of your gear. With experience, practice and

The diver **above** feels like he's gliding through the air as he easily and weightlessly passes along an underwater cliff, admiring the finger sponges, soft corals and other life that grow out from the wall. On the **right,** a diver drifts over a mound of plate corals, savoring the peace and the quiet of the undersea world.

training, becoming neutrally buoyant will become second nature to you. And what a thrill to be "light as a feather!"

Silence

The underwater environment is mostly a silent world. Your exhaust bubbles, however, are your constant companion. If you stop hearing them, you're out of air, a topic we'll get into later.

There are a few other sounds down there, too. Among them are the crunchings of parrotfish as they chew up coral for the tiny food they contain. (As parrotfish digest the coral, they excrete fine sand, which accounts for many of the world's beaches.) Other fish make grunts and some shrimp make a popping sound with their claws. Another sound you'll come across now and then is the metallic rapping of a dive knife against an air cylinder as your dive guide or a partner taps to get your attention. Sometimes, too, the operators of the boat from which you might be diving will signal to the divers by banging on its side, letting everyone know to come to the surface for one reason or another.

You can hear people yell underwater also, if they're trying to get your attention.

Color

Ever wonder what life would look like if you were color blind? That's how things look underwater—sort of like old black-and-white movies on TV, but with a little blue thrown in.

You see, water absorbs colors, starting with vivid ones such as red and orange. If you're diving on a bright day with plenty of light, colors will appear normal within the first ten feet or so. But as you descend, the red turns to black, and at thirty feet there's no more orange. By the time you reach sixty feet, yellow disappears. Green, the last color to go, looks gray around eighty feet. Aside from various shades of gray, you're usually left with only blue. Blue is with you always, except during night dives.

Restoring color, though, is simple. An inexpensive underwater flashlight will do the job. If you shine your light on, for example, a dark gray sponge, it'll leap to life in red, orange, brown or whatever its natural color is. At least ninety percent of the underwater photos you see in books or magazines are taken with underwater strobe lights just for this reason—to restore the scene's actual colors long enough to take a picture.

Above a couple of divers cruise the bottom at seventy feet in a blue world, since the water has filtered out the sun's light so much that we can't see any bright colors at this depth. For instance, the barrel sponge on the **upper right** appears to be a dull brownish-gray, while the **lower** one glows its natural color when spotted with an underwater flashlight. On the **left**, a bright red sponge reaches up from a yellow and white coral head as yellow and black sergeant major fish scurry about—but, at sixty feet down you couldn't see the colors without a light.

Water

Even with the best protective clothing, you'll feel the water's temperature. You might be diving in a fifty-degree lake all snug in your wet suit and rubber gloves, but water will sneak in from somewhere, maybe briefly running down your neck and back. You'll shiver for a second until your body temperature heats the water and you no longer notice the chill. Your face can get cold too, but the sensation is

soon forgotten until you come to the surface again, get out of your gear and realize how chilly you really are.

Besides cold and warm, water can also be rough or calm. In rough water, you'll feel yourself pushed here or there, and you'll have to take that into account when planning where you're going and how you'll get back to your boat. Drift diving is a method some people use in strong currents. You hop into the water, go below to your agreed-upon depth, then let the water take you along at its own pace. While you're drifting, the dive boat will move down current, so that when you come to the surface at the end of your dive, there it is.

But rough water and drift diving are only for the more experienced divers.

*At **left** a diver explores a typical coral scene. **Above** is an inverted starfish, one of the countless small animals waiting to be discovered by divers.*

Depth

Depth fascinates every beginning diver. The safe maximum recreational diving depth is around one hundred thirty feet. And most divers are satisfied with that, because if you go much deeper, the visibility diminishes, your allowable time down there is greatly limited (often just ten minutes or less) and usually, there simply isn't as much interesting stuff to see.

Experienced divers will tell you that the best average dives are fifty feet or less. You have more light, more animals, and you can possibly stay down well over an hour. And at thirty feet, you're only limited by the amount of air in your scuba tank.

Deep-diving sounds challenging, adventurous, even dangerous. It's all of those, but leave it to the professionals. For a safe, long, fun dive, spend most of your time at fifty feet or less.

*To the **left**, just forty feet below the surface is a world of tube sponges and staghorn corals. You don't have to go deep to enjoy the underwater world. The snorkeler **below**, only ten feet deep, explores a coral head packed with thousands of living creatures.*

Above is a curious French angelfish, one of the common inhabitants of the coral reef. At the **top right** is a porcupinefish that has puffed itself up with water to possibly scare off the photographer. *Next* is a moray eel. They can be dangerous if frightened or if they mistake your fingers for food, but otherwise, these shy creatures just hover around their coral holes, minding their own business (unless it's nighttime when they come out in search of meals). The **next** photo shows a diver holding a sea cucumber which normally crawls very slowly along the ocean floor, doing what most underwater life does most of the time — looking for something to eat. To the **right** is a trumpetfish that can usually be found swimming vertically among the hard and soft corals.

Animals

What will you see down there? As we mentioned, there's plenty of plant-like animal life. But, of course, there are also fish—lots of them in all different sizes, shapes and colors. You might notice tiny, brilliantly-colored ones first. You may also see somewhat larger varieties, and if you get lucky, you might spot some gigantic ones.

Some are flat, others long and snake-like. There are oval fish, circular fish, round fish, needle-shaped fish, box-like fish. Some are so camouflaged you'll probably never spot them, while others stand out in neon. There are creatures that look like worms, and others that resemble slugs and snails.

There are also crabs of all types, plus lobsters, abalone, clams, and a million other critters. They seem to be simply waiting for you to float by and take a peek, though many are so shy you'll have to be very still and patient to get a look.

Naturally you'll see sand and rocks, but there are many other geologic wonders down there, such as walls of under-water cliffs that drop thousands of feet below the surface. Many are lined with

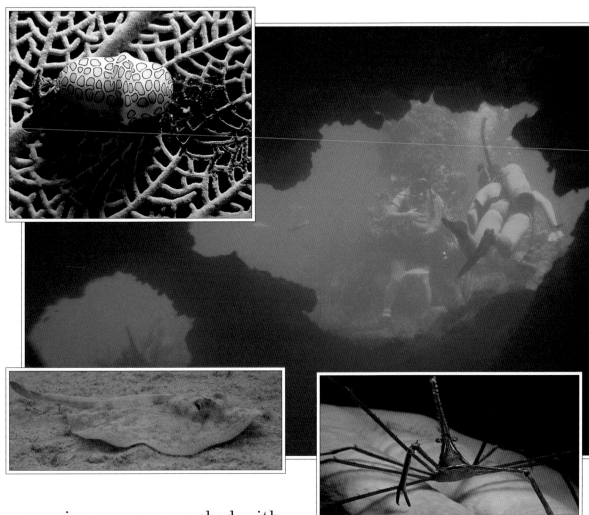

massive sponges, cracked with huge valleys and pierced by winding tunnels. Some locations possess coral reefs made by millions of microscopic animals that stretch for thousands of miles. Other reefs may only be a few hundred feet.

And then, there are shells: big ones, small ones, dull, mottled ones, and ones you'd swear had been hand-painted. Often you'll spot shells that seem to "walk" past, because creatures such as hermit crabs have taken up residence in abandoned shells. At other times you'll see a a beautiful conch (pronounced "conk") shell sliding along as the snail-like creature inside sneaks its "foot" out, grabs some of the sandy floor, and drags the rest of its body and shell along with it. Shells are terrific to collect, but remember, most of the ones you'll see are actually homes to living animals, so treat them gently, and put them back if you've moved them. There are more than 70,000 kinds of shells, so you certainly won't get bored.

Facing page: Swimming through underwater tunnels is a thrill because of the many things you see, like corals and sponges lining the walls. On the **facing page top left** is a one-inch flamingo tongue snail, shown here having eaten part of a sea fan. It's covered by a thin spotted membrane. When it's disturbed, it slowly pulls its colorful jacket inside, leaving only its plain cream-colored shell visible. On the **facing page bottom left** a stingray lies motionless on the bottom, blending in with the color and texture of the sand, hoping it won't be seen. Some rays will actually flip sand over themselves, so that merely their eyes are visible. On the **facing page bottom right** is an arrow crab, which is so small and delicate it can stand in your open palm. On **this page above** a slimy brittle star, one of the many types of starfish with a body only one inch in diameter, rests on a clump of hard coral (the bright streaks in the background are actually minuscule creatures caught by the camera's strobe light in fleeting motion). To the **top left** is a hermit crab that uses abandoned shells to make its home. In the **center** an abandoned conch shell lies on the sand. At the **bottom** is a lobster that can often be found hiding in crevices and under ledges during the day. At night they come out to forage.

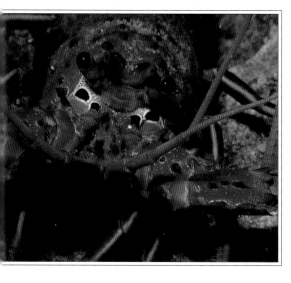

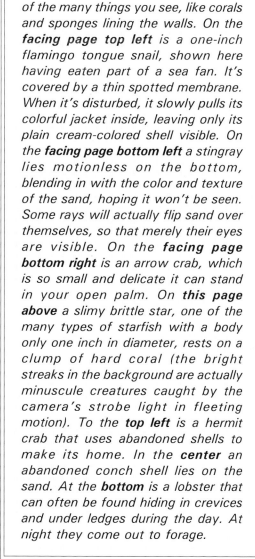

Shipwrecks

Every diver dreams of coming upon an old shipwreck. The world's oceans are literally filled with them, but unfortunately there is only a relative handful that are within the depths of safe diving. Even so, most dive guides know where to take their customers. If wrecks are what fascinate you, all you have to do is let the guides know. When diving a wreck, don't grab for souvenirs; leave them for other divers to equally enjoy.

There are destroyed military vessels and even airplanes, sunken cargo ships, old fishing boats and a whole lot more. Some you can even dive inside of, exploring rooms and compartments as though you were the first person ever there.

Top left: Some of the world's wrecks lie so shallow that even breath-holding snorkelers can dive down to them. To the **middle left** a solitary anchor lies in the sand. At the **bottom left** is a large tanker that ran aground on a Caribbean reef during a hurricane. As it continued to rust and weaken over the years, another hurricane broke it in two. Diving below wrecks like this can be very dangerous, since there's no predicting when more of it will crumble as the saltwater takes its toll on the metal. The perfect wrecks for scuba divers, however, are like the one **above**, where an entire ship rests deep enough so surface conditions don't destroy it, and where its equipment and rooms are almost fully intact.

Is diving dangerous?

It can be, but so can driving, skateboarding, or bike riding. You can minimize the risks with all these activities as long as you are careful, pay attention, and go by the rules.

Nothing underwater will go out of its way to harm you. Think about it: If you were confronted by a creature you'd never seen before, one that was two to twenty times larger than yourself, with bubbles spewing forth and things hanging all over it, what would you do? Attack? Not likely. You'd get out of there fast. And that's what most underwater animals do.

Divers usually get hurt when they don't think. They reach into some dark hole feeling for lobster, and scare a sleeping moray eel that defends itself with its razor-sharp teeth. Or they crawl along on the sand floor instead of gliding above it, and bump into a spiny urchin with piercing needles—needles that are used only to protect itself. Some divers carelessly bang into jagged corals and get scraped or crash into aboat's swim platform and get bruised.

*The spotted moray **above** looks menacing with its mouth open, but that is how morays breathe. **Below** is a green moray eel. Sure, its teeth are plenty sharp, but morays are shy, and much more interested in a bite of fish than a bite of a finger.*

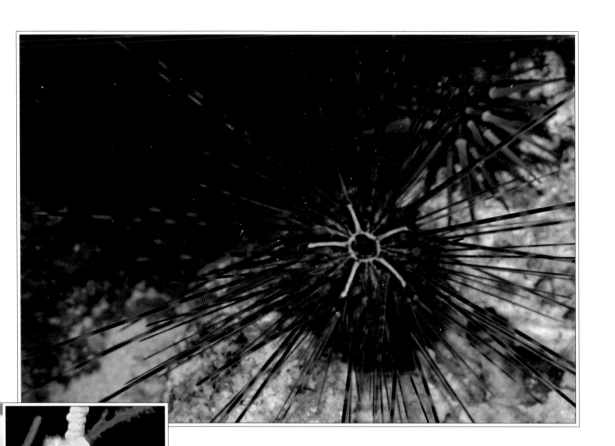

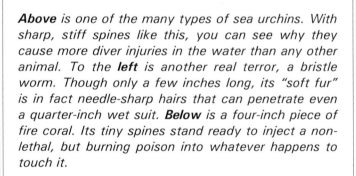

Above is one of the many types of sea urchins. With sharp, stiff spines like this, you can see why they cause more diver injuries in the water than any other animal. To the **left** is another real terror, a bristle worm. Though only a few inches long, its "soft fur" is in fact needle-sharp hairs that can penetrate even a quarter-inch wet suit. **Below** is a four-inch piece of fire coral. Its tiny spines stand ready to inject a non-lethal, but burning poison into whatever happens to touch it.

*A blue shark at **top** is one of more than 350 types of sharks, with only a handful dangerous to man. This one will take a nip if it's provoked, but will just glide past if left alone. **Above** is the ultimate fear — the great white shark. But they are so seldom seen that, worldwide, they may attack only three or four humans in an entire year.*

Sharks? That's what every non-diver worries about, and every diver lusts for. Divers are thrilled when they see a shark. After all, divers know that more people are killed by bee stings in a year than are killed are sharks. You're more likely to be struck by lightning than bit by a shark. Generally, sharks aren't as interested in you as you are in them. After all they're going about their business, like everything else down there.

Some jellyfish can cause serious stings. Lionfish, a beautiful but extremely rare animal, can do the same. Some creatures, like the ugly, but even rarer stonefish, can cause a sting that may kill you. In a year, worldwide, there may be only one or two deaths by these guys, though.

But not all hazards in scuba diving have fins or gills. Take, for instance, running out of air. It's rare, but it can happen. And divers have to be prepared for it. Occasionally, the equipment can be at fault. Perhaps there's a leak in one of the hoses behind your head where you can't see or hear it, though your buddy or someone else you're diving with should spot the bubbles and signal you. But equipment doesn't mess up nearly as often as people do, and that's where the out-of-air situation usually comes from—from a diver not paying attention to his air gauge.

What happens when you do run out? You can signal to your dive buddy, and then either share his air by alternating breaths off his mouthpiece, or by using his extra emergency regulator hose and mouthpiece (called an "octopus") which is attached to his air tank, as you both slowly ascend to the surface. There are even small bottles of extra air that you can strap to your body or equipment, just in case. But you'll learn all about sharing air in your scuba class, and you even won't mind when your instructor briefly turns your air off so you learn what to expect!

Let's glance at a few other dangers that divers have to deal with. Getting lost is one. If you're gazing around at the beauty and life, and not paying attention to where the boat is or where you entered on the beach, you could be in for a surprise. At the end of the dive, you could come up only to find the boat a couple of hundred yards away, or that you've drifted far from where you need to be.

You can also be in trouble if you snag your gear on rocks, coral, or sharp edges of submerged wrecks. This might rip the mouthpiece right out of your mouth, tear your mask off, or even snare you to where you can't get free without the help of your buddy or another diver.

Another way divers can become injured is by taking a breath of air underwater and ascending while holding their breath. As you rise there is less pressure so the air in your lungs expands. It has to have some place to go, so if you are not exhaling, the air can escape by rupturing a portion of your lung wall. Serious stuff, but the cardinal rule of "never hold your breath" will be drummed into you over and over during training until it becomes second nature.

Coming to the surface too

quickly is also a danger. You'll learn in your scuba classes that when breathing air from tanks underwater, your body absorbs a gas called nitrogen. The deeper you go and the longer you stay down, the more nitrogen you absorb. It goes away on its own as you come slowly to the water's surface and rest on the boat or shore after a dive. But what happens when you go up faster than you were taught? Sometimes the nitrogen doesn't have time to leave your body and gas bubbles get stuck, most often in your joints. That can hurt a lot and the joint cramps up on you. That's why they call this problem "the bends."

Then there's nitrogen narcosis—the rapture of the deep. At depths below 100 feet or so, some divers will start to feel a little giddy. Everything seems more beautiful than ever, and you feel like you could stay there the rest of your life. Checking your gauges for air or depth is the furthest thing from your mind and that can have serious consequences. When divers do have to dive deep for work or rescue, they have special training, and often breathe unique mixed gasses rather than just air that's in the usual scuba tank.

You've also got to notice the current so you don't drift away,

the temperature so you don't get too cold to be safe, and changes in the weather so you don't come up to a raging storm. With training and experience, you'll be confident enough so you won't panic if something seems weird. You should do some sort of regular exercise to stay in shape so you won't get so exhausted you can't swim back when the dive is over.

As you can see from this list of dangers, most of the problems in scuba diving come from ourselves. Some of us forget or neglect the basic rules of safe diving we learned when we started out. We hold our breaths when going to the surface; we forget to check our gauges for our depth and air in our tank; we panic when we have a problem instead of calmly analyzing the situation and solving it. All scuba divers have to remember the safety rules, be attentive, and use properly maintained equipment. And, as the old saying goes, plan your dive, then dive your plan.

GETTING STARTED

Back before Cousteau and Gagnon invented the scuba regulator system we all know now, people still dove with tanks. Many modified fire department equipment for underwater. These hearty, maybe even foolhardy, souls were blazing the trail. They were also getting hurt.

They didn't know about nitrogen bubbles; they didn't have even basic gauges, let alone computers, to tell them what was going on. They didn't have the Navy dive charts that have become the standard way of measuring how deep to go for how many minutes and when it was safe to dive next. Many got the "bends," and some even became paralyzed from it.

These pioneers of the 50's and early 60's didn't have much choice. Today, however, we have it easy. We have classes that teach us how it all works, and how to do it safely.

The two most common

> *Scuba classes generally start in the dive shop, sometimes with a small student-to-teacher ratio, other times in a room with a dozen or more.*

courses are the resort course and the basic open water certification course. The resort course is a simple introduction to scuba diving, and has its limits as we'll explore in a minute. The open water class, on the other hand, gives you a certification card (called a C-card) that you must show when you rent equipment, get your air tanks filled, and dive from a dive boat. By checking the C-card, diving professionals can be certain that the person is a qualified diver and not likely to hurt themselves or endanger others.

A good way to get an introduction to diving is by snorkeling. Instruction for snorkeling is covered in a basic scuba course, but one does not have to be a certified diver to enjoy the sport.

Snorkeling

Snorkeling—gliding along the water's surface with a plastic breathing tube in your mouth, and wearing fins, a mask and sometimes an inflated vest—is the world's sixth fastest growing sport with millions of participants.

Snorkeling can be done in all waters—lakes, reservoirs, oceans and rivers—but it is less safe in rough waters. People even snorkel in near freezing waters, but of course they are properly protected from the chilling temperatures.

While snorkeling is a popular recreation, it can be a lot more. In order to protect much of the water's creatures, many parts of the world prohibit gathering food while on scuba, but allow it while snorkeling, giving the fish and shellfish of the earth a fair chance of survival. And what if your motor boat gets its prop tangled in seaweed and has to be freed. Snorkeling can come in real handy.

Even you aren't a trained scuba diver, you can still experience the beauty and wonder of the underwater world by snorkeling. It's a pretty simple procedure, actually. Have you ever seen those old war movies where escaped captives hide from their pursuers under jungle swamp water by breathing from broken-off reed tubes? It's the same idea. In snorkeling, you hold a plastic tube (the snorkel) in your mouth as you slowly swim along on the water's surface. The tube is bent back over your head so the top sticks up a few inches into the air. You've also got a mask on so you can see underwater without hassle or irritation. And with lightly

These photos illustrate some common warm water sights for snorkelers. **Left**, a curious gray angelfish investigates the photographer. **Above**, a cluster of tiny, graceful tube worms wave in the slight current.

flexible fins on your feet, you can kick along effortlessly. By using an inflated vest, you can stay afloat for long periods tirelessly.

If the water is cold, you'll have on either a lightweight nylon suit or, if it's real cold, you'll more than likely be dressed in a rubber wet suit. Even if the water is very warm, wearing some clothes can still be a good idea. Remember that sun. Spending all day cruising along with only an inch or two of water covering your back is a perfect way to get sunburn. So unless you have a good tan, you'll be well advised to wear a t-shirt and lightweight pants along with a whole lot of waterproof sunscreen.

Another safety consideration is motor boats. The drivers skip along the surface of the water, sometimes at blazing speeds, and they're not watching out for snorkelers. You should either stay away from waters with heavy boat traffic, or have a floatable dive flag with you. This is usually a red flag with a white diagonal stripe. It floats at the surface by a plastic balloon or circular tube, and may be either tied to a weight on the bottom or even to your ankle. This way boaters will see the flag long before they can see you. The best idea is to stay on the beach if there are boats in the water.

Current is another thing snorkelers have to think about as well. The strongest and most frequent currents are on the surface where snorkelers are. Scuba divers have less of a problem with current, because after the first ten feet under the surface, most currents are either less strong or have vanished completely. You either skip a day in the water, or start out by swimming strongly against the current so that as you snorkel, the water will then bring you back towards where you started the dive.

Can you really enjoy yourself snorkeling? Absolutely! Water magnifies, so that what you see seems larger and closer than it actually is. As you coast along, lightly kicking your fins, arms at your side for streamlining, you'll be amazed at what you can see, especially if you're in water that's only ten to twenty feet deep. At

that depth, there is plenty of sunlight to brighten the scene. And when you see something particularly interesting, you can easily hold your breath and dive down to the bottom for a much closer look.

When diving to the bottom, water will go down the opening of your snorkel, but that's no problem. When you float back to the surface, you blow through the tube, blasting the water back out the top. Some snorkels are self-draining, but there's almost always a bit of water left. A simple puff will clear it out.

Snorkeling is easy, it's cheap, and it's fun. It's also the ideal way to see if you'd like to go ahead and learn to scuba dive.

The Resort Course

This is simply an introduction to scuba diving which, when completed, allows you to go on a supervised open water dive. Let's say that you like the idea of diving, but are a little concerned about how your ears will feel, if you'll get claustrophobic, or about your athletic ability.

For less than $100 you can sample this fascinating sport of scuba diving. The course includes about an hour of classroom teaching. You learn why it is dangerous to hold your breath while coming to the surface, and why you should ascend slowly. The instructor introduces you to all the equipment, explaining what it's for, how to use it, how to take care of it, and what to do if any of it stops working right.

A few scuba mechanical skills are demonstrated too, like how to safely get water out your mask in case it leaks. And you learn to master your buoyancy so that you aren't so heavy you're smashing onto the coral, or so light you're zooming up to the surface.

Then it's off to a pool or some shallow, clear water at the beach. Over the next hour or two you learn to master mask-clearing, experiment with a tank on your back and a mouthpiece feeding you air as you inhale, and generally get comfortable with the gear

Scuba equipment may seem like a puzzle at first, but after proper training it's as natural as suiting up for any of your favorite sports.

and the new environment.

Then you're ready for your first actual scuba dive. Because you aren't fully certified yet, you're permitted to dive only with an instructor, and only to a limited depth of about 40 feet. These restrictions are for your own safety. Remember, you've only gained a fraction of the knowledge that certified divers have, and no one wants anything to go wrong. But, at least you're diving.

Generally, a resort course includes only one dive. But you're sure to be hooked and want more, so the next step is to get certified.

Open Water Certification

The full certification is like a resort course, only it goes into much more detail. And there are tests. If you want to become a scuba diver, you have to learn to be self-reliant when the time comes, to help your fellow divers if the need arises, and to safely enjoy everything the sport offers.

Open water certification classes run from four to six days, depending on the number of other students, the instructor's and your available time, how hard you study, and how well you learn.

You find out a whole lot

more about what to do when something goes wrong, such as a weightbelt falling off, or getting stung by a jellyfish, or running out of air. You're told about expanding gasses in your body, and taught how to care for the fragile underwater environment.

There's a bunch more, like how to safely enter the water and gracefully get back out. You find out all that your equipment does for you and how to properly keep it working right.

The diver to the **left** is about to use a "giant stride" which you'll learn in your course to enter the water from a dive boat. The water sessions is where the real fun starts. **Above** instructors take a group to a shallow, sandy area to review skills learned in the pool. Note that these divers are dressed for cold water. Photo by Roberta Poole-Crockett.

The water skills are more advanced, too. You're tested on taking off the buoyancy vest and tank, then putting it back on—underwater. You learn to control your buoyancy, your level of lift and drop, as you rise and fall with each breath you take below the surface. You're taught how to avoid getting lost and how to help someone who is.

And you're tested more than once. Remember, no one is trying to hassle you; the instructor wants you to be-come a safe diver, a confident diver, and a helpful diver. When it's all over, you are awarded your C-card.

These classes are generally conducted by certified instructors at dive shops, in college or night schools, and even at the local YMCA. The prices can vary, depending on whether or not equipment use is included, and if you're in a large group or by yourself with the instructor.

Certifications are overseen by various sanctioning organizations who have perfected the teaching materials and training methods.

Advanced Training

You can continue your education, too, if you like what you've gotten into, and want to learn more.

For one thing, there's an advanced open water course. Then, there are a bunch of specialty courses, such as wreck diving, photography, cave diving, medic first aid, rescue diver, underwater naturalist, search and rescue diver, and later, divemaster, instructor, master instructor, and more.

EQUIPMENT

Scuba diving is a technology sport requiring the use of some pretty sophisticated equipment. Here are some of the basics.

Masks

Masks keep the water out of your eyes and give you a pocket of air which allows you to see clearly underwater. There are generally two types: one with a lens for each eye, and another with a single clear plate across your face. Most divers like the second version, but if you normally wear glasses, it's easier and better-looking to use the two-lens variety with corrected-vision lenses installed.

The main consideration when picking a mask is fit. The rubber or silicone plastic around the lens should be smooth and soft, preferably clear so you won't feel closed in. The strap must be one that'll hold the mask firmly in place without putting you in a headlock. The mask should also match the shape of your face, that is, not too narrow and not too wide, or it will leak. All scuba masks have a nose pocket you can pinch

*As you can see from the picture **above** of a typical set of dive gear, scuba is an equipment intensive sport. Part of your open water course will be devoted to using and taking care of dive equipment.*

from the outside to relieve the pressure in your ear underwater.

Snorkels

A snorkel for scuba diving? You bet! There are times a snorkel comes in real handy.

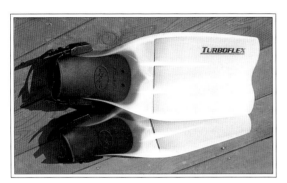

For instance when you want to save your air and swim out to the location you want to dive down to. Or if you run out of air at the surface in real choppy water and have to either wait for help or swim to the shore or boat.

Fins

Fins, of course, are what help propel you through the water. They come in all shapes, colors and sizes. As with masks, though, comfort is the thing. They all pretty much act the same way, by bending when you kick, then straightening out to push you through the water.

There are full-foot models and open-foot ones with straps. Those with straps are adjustable, and allow for wet suit boots which keep your feet warm and prevent the fins from rubbing your feet and toes raw.

Buoyancy Compensator

The BC or BCD (buoyancy compensator device) is a treat. You can inflate it by either blowing into it through a tube or by pressing a button to send a bit of air in from your tank. Press another button or pull a cord and it deflates.

All this allows you to fine-tune your level of buoyancy so that you can remain neutral instead of sinking if you accidentally over-weighted yourself.

At the water's surface, you can pump more air into the BC so you can float effortlessly if you're waiting for your friends or for a rescue. Speaking of rescue, if you have to assist a troubled diver, inflating *his* BC and keeping him on the surface can save his life.

Your instructor will teach you that since air expands as you rise toward the surface, you've got to be able to let the air *out* of the BC as you go up, or the expanding air will make you more and more buoyant and you will go faster and faster. Rising too fast is not safe ascent and can cause a number of problems.

BCs have other benefits besides helping to control buoyancy. They have pockets for storing such things as lights and underwater slates for making notes. Also, the vest comes with plenty of clips

Below is the entire regulator setup with your mouthpiece, the octopus mouthpiece, the valve that screws on to the tank, a hose that connects to your BC, and a console containing an air pressure gauge and depth gauge. To the *left* is a close-up of your main regulator and mouthpiece.

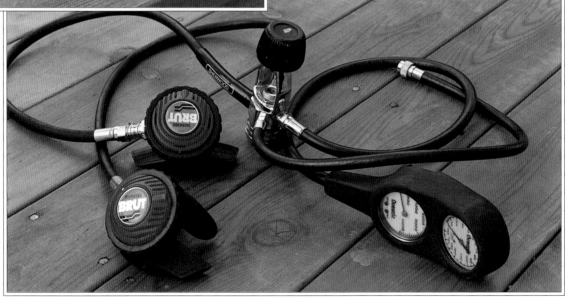

for hanging stuff.

Like with every other piece of gear these days, BCs come in a variety of styles and colors. Just stick with a well-known brand.

Regulators and Gauges

The regulator is the hose device that runs from the top of the tank to your mouth. Air flows through it only when you inhale or exhale. It functions when you demand it to, so it's generally referred to as a "demand" regulator.

Attached to this is often a second regulator, an "octopus,"

that either floats along behind your tank or is lightly attached to your BC. The octopus is used when another diver runs out of air and needs to breathe off your tank as you take him or her to the surface. Many of the newer BCs, however, have what's called an alternate air source, a tube fixed to the front of your vest so you can breathe from your tank through it while handing your regulator to your out-of-air buddy.

There's another hose that's part of the regulator system, and it attaches from the tank to your air pressure gauge.

This gauge simply shows you how much air you have left. Let's say you start a dive with 3,000 pounds per square inch (psi, as its called, is a method of measuring air in your tank). As you dive, you regularly check this gauge to see how much you're using and how much is left.

There's also a gauge to show you your depth, called, simply, a depth gauge. It indicates how many feet you are below the surface. As with the pressure gauge, it operates automatically.

These gauges are contained in a single unit known as a console, so everything you need to

> **Below** is a sampling of digital computers which are becoming increasingly popular. Some models can tell you how long you can stay underwater without getting the bends and measure time, depth and air consumption.

watch is together. Usually, there's room for a compass and a "bottom-timer." The bottom-timer turns on automatically at a certain depth and keeps track of how long you've been underwater.

A new and exciting trend in diving equipment has been the advent of dive computers. Battery-powered, they take the place of numerous gauges and monitor your depth, time, air pressure, water temperature and more. Computers take into account your various depths during your dive, and tell you how much nitrogen you have absorbed and how long you can stay down. Some computers are quite basic while others are very complicated. Dive computers are becoming almost standard equipment these days.

Exposure Suits

Some "wet suits" can be thick enough to keep you warm under ice, while others are "skins," so thin you hardly feel them. What you wear depends on water conditions and your own temperature comfort zone. Many wet suits come with hoods to keep your head warm and prevent it from losing your body's natural heat. They can also protect you from nasty cuts underwater.

For super-cold diving, most people wear a "dry suit" that contains air to keep the diver insulated from the water's temperature and even keeps him dry.

Boots

As we mentioned earlier, boots keep your fins from rubbing your feet too much.

Boots also come in differing thicknesses, again depending on the warmth you need in the water you're diving. And boots, like nearly everything else, come in numerous colors and styles.

A main consideration when buying boots is how easy they are to put on. Some come with zippers, although zippers can deteriorate with years of neglect. The other choice, of course, is boots without zippers, but getting those on and off can be frustrating. Go with the zippers.

Another consideration are the soles. If you are going to be walking to the water over a rocky beach, you'll want to have enough protection.

Weight Belts

These belts range from a tough canvas or rubber belt on which you thread your lead weights to help keep you down, to a more comfortable soft neoprene one with pockets into which you slip the weights. Some newer BC's even have weight pockets.

Additional Items

Dive knives. They generally come in two styles—those for cutting and those for prying. The prying ones don't have points. Most beginning divers think they need a knife to protect themselves from the evils of the deep. On the contrary, their main use is to cut yourself out of seaweed or old fishing line if you get entangled.

You can also use a knife to tap on your tank (sound travels well underwater) to get someone's attention.

In most cases, especially in the clear, warm water of the tropics, they aren't really necessary. But they sure look good, strapped to your leg.

Tanks. You don't have to own one unless you're diving where few other people go. You

At **left** is a common wet suit with vest for maximum protection. **Below left** are zippered boots. **Below** is a typical tank capable of holding a few thousand pounds of compressed air.

will usually dive where there are dive shops around, and it's easy to simply rent a tank from them for the day. Naturally, you have to show your C-card. Rental is very reasonable, especially when you consider the alternative of hauling a steel or aluminum tank around with you. Your other gear is heavy enough. Save your energy for the dive.

Camera equipment. If you've been diving a while, you may want your own still camera, movie camera, or video camera. More to pack and lug, but they sure can be a lot of fun.

Care and Maintenance

Saltwater and equipment don't get along very well. Any water is tough on your gear, and so is sunlight and blowing sand.

Don't forget, this equipment is keeping you from serious injury, maybe even death. If you were a skydiver, you'd sure take care of that parachute, wouldn't you? If you want all your dive gear to work right, you've got to keep it clean, salt-free, and properly maintained. You should check all your gear before every dive to make sure everything works right.

Those courses we referred to earlier will also cover equip-ment maintenance. This is as important a topic as running out of air, so pay attention.

Make sure your gear is always packed and stored properly, and that you service it at the right intervals or after every dive trip.

Where to get it all? You've probably seen those lovely scuba displays in your favorite sporting goods store or depart-ment store. But you aren't likely to find a salesperson who's a diver or knows a BC from a boot. It's okay to buy a basketball from these guys, but not a breathing regulator.

Stick to the dive shops. Diving and dive equipment is what these guys do for a living. They're pros. They deal with this stuff everyday, and can steer you through the selection of gear that's right for your needs.

That's about it for equip-ment basics. There's much more, of course. But with time and experience, you'll figure out if you really need that lift bag that hauls heavy items from the ocean floor, or that floating dive flag or that infla-table raft or....

WHERE DO PEOPLE DIVE?

Anywhere there's water you'll find divers. Those who live near the ocean certainly dive there. But what about those who live, say, in the middle of the U.S. where the closest open water is perhaps a thousand miles away? Fine for a vacation, but not for a weekend dip. Here divers will head for a lake or even a smoothly-flowing river if it's not too swift. Sometimes these places are murky or even kind of muddy, but no matter. A diver wants to dive, wants to get geared up and be underwater.

Others will find a local reservoir or an old quarry. These can be great for diving. The water is usually clear, but rather cold. Often there are plenty of fish to see and photograph. And some reservoirs were even created over old abandoned villages so that divers can swim through ghostly houses and investigate.

Suppose you live in Alaska? The water is well below freezing in places like that. Divers, wearing highly protective clothing and special dive equipment, will simply chop holes in the ice and drop down. It's dangerous, however. Not just because of the temperature that can freeze the body as well as the regulator, but because of the ice cover. Cave diving is even more specialized, and divers will pack their gear many miles into the jungle to dive caves like those found in Mexico.

You get the idea, divers dive. Sure, most would like to be in the tropical waters where visibility and temperature are over 80. Still, there are those who'd pass up a free plane ticket to the Caribbean in order to break a hole in the ice somewhere.

SPECIALTY DIVING

Not all scuba divers just want to look around. Some make careers out of various types of diving, such as search and rescue work or underwater construction. We'll get into some of the diving careers in the next chapter.

For recreational divers, there are many other types of specialized diving, like cave diving and wreck diving. Let's take a look at the most popular kinds of specialty diving.

Photography

This one's the most popular. More divers go into underwater photography than any other sort of specialty diving.

For most divers, still photography or underwater videography are simply nice ways to

---

Below, a diver enters the water using the favorite entry of almost all boat divers—the giant stride. At **right**, a photographer lines up a shot.

bring further enjoyment to an already pleasant hobby. Get decent at it and you can show your work to friends who've never tried scuba, or you can blow up your best photos and display them on your walls. There are even contests, some paying hefty prize money or handsome certificates.

Once you start taking pictures on your dives, it's hard to stop. After you get the bug, every dive will consist of searching for interesting critters, perfect compositions, and ideal light—whether or not you have your camera with you. You'll be seeing sea life in totally new ways, with a more detail-oriented eye. And you'll learn more about the underwater world, too, because in order to get the best animal photos and videos, you'll have to learn their daytime and nighttime habits—how they move, what they eat and where they live.

Taking underwater pictures can also be a frustrating project. The day you set up your camera equipment for extreme closeups is the day a huge ray will glide right next to you, or when you've planned on taking those big scenes the most colorful one-inch shrimp

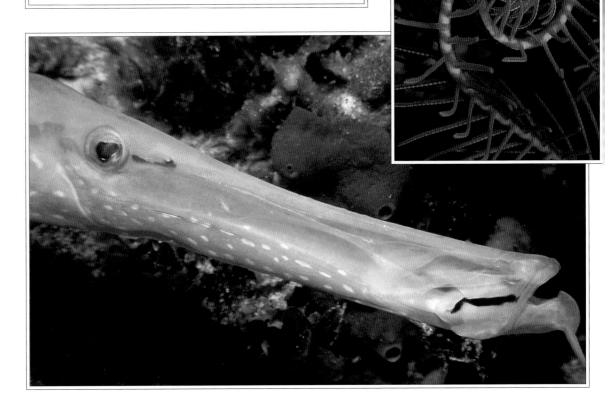

With close-focusing lenses, photographers can capture a variety of marine animals. **Below** is the face of a three-foot long trumpetfish. They use their long, narrow snouts to suck in unsuspecting prey. At **right** is a three-inch long crinoid also called a feather star. At night they extend their long arms to capture small planktonic organisms. The crinoid, like the trumpetfish, come in a variety of colors.

of your life will come along. The problem is that with most cameras you can't change lenses underwater. You're stuck with what you brought into the water with you. You have the best film for a bright, sunny day, and the clouds will drift in front of the sun just as you're ready to snap the camera shutter. Full-time professionals will dive with two, three, or even more cameras, all with different lenses and different film, just in case.

As you can guess, getting into still photography, film or video can be rather expensive. But it doesn't have to be, especially if you're just getting started and learning what it's all about. A few hundred dollars or less will get you going. And now there are automatic cameras that'll give you real good, if not professional-quality, pictures every time. For ten or twenty dollars you can buy cameras that are perfect for snorkeling, though you can't take them much below ten feet.

With time and experience, you can get more sophisticated equipment and take more sophisticated photos or videos. After all, this is how almost every great pro started out.

Night Diving

After photography and videography, night diving is the most widely done specialty.

"Dive at night? You've got to be kidding!" An all too frequent response from the beginner or the non-diver. People who don't know, think this is when all the bad stuff comes out, the animals that lie in wait to do unspeakable nasties to unsuspecting divers.

Many animals do come out at night in search of food, but they aren't about to attack something a whole lot bigger than themselves. Other animals are sleeping under ledges or in crevices, or drifting along with the current.

How does night diving work? Typically, a diver will attach a small light to his tank so others will know where he or she is. And as you might imagine, an underwater flashlight is a must on a night dive. Without one you miss everything. It's mighty dark down there. With a light, everything you shine it on comes to colorful life. You'll see sleeping fish, some soft, flower-like corals that "blossom" as their tiny

At night many animals leave their daytime hiding places to forage for food. Here the author spots a crab during a night dive. Photo by Joe Stebbins.

tentacles reach out to filter invisible bits of food from the water, and little creatures that hide during the day.

Scary? Nah. Exciting? Yes indeed.

Wreck Diving

What a thrill, easing around a sunken vehicle or slipping into a submerged ship. For one thing, wrecks are mysterious. For another, the sea life loves to take over wrecks. Plants and corals will grow on the wreck's surfaces and attract fish and invertebrates. Even on a sandy bottom, a shipwreck will become an oasis of life.

Wrecks are mysterious, but they're also potentially dangerous—at least some are. Find a sunken ship and the chances are good that you'll also find jagged rusting metal that can cause nasty cuts to

you or your equipment. On some wrecks it is also easy to get lost inside and never find your way out.

Occasionally, divers have taken a useless ship or even a car and intentionally sunk it to provide a dive site. As the underwater growth takes over, a perfect man-made reef becomes available for divers and photographers to enjoy for years to come.

Some wrecks are too deep for diving, being well below the maximum recommended sport diving depth of one hundred thirty feet. Still, there are plenty, all over the world, that are just fifteen to fifty feet down, looking eerie, even ghostly, in their blue-green surroundings, and just waiting for you to visit.

Research

Underwater scientific or industrial research can make a tremendously valuable contribution to the world.

You may be linked with an organization examining behavior patterns of everything from whales to starfish, noting on underwater slates where they live, how they move about, what they eat, how they sleep, and how they mate.

There's underwater archaeology, too, where divers investigate submerged ruins of earlier civilizations or ancient ships. You photograph them, or plot the location of parts that will later be raised and reconstructed. You clean debris and growth away, make underwater drawings and record your observations.

Researchers may even

ignore the obvious sea life to focus their efforts on the water itself, taking samples to be analyzed for chemicals, pollutants or waste content.

Ice Diving

We looked a little at ice diving earlier. This one takes plenty of diving experience and special training. It's dangerous. There's the temperature, of course, that can shut down normal regulators and

A research diver, **left**, protected by a chain metal suit like the knights of old, prepares to check out behavior patterns of sharks. **Below**, the researcher and the metal suit at work. Both survived.

penetrate normal wet suits. There's also the danger of not finding your way back to the opening. However, with careful training, detailed planning and specialized gear, ice diving can provide some of the most beautiful sights of the underwater world.

Cave Diving

We also touched on underwater cave diving. This one is among the most hazardous the scuba world offers. For one thing, there's silt. Silt is super-fine dirt that's collected over the years on the floor and also the roof of these caves. It's dark in there, naturally, but lights can take care of that. However, bump into the top of the cave or kick your fins a little too hard and all that silt gets stirred up, dropping visibility to zero. Even the strongest light you can buy is useless.

Cave divers, after plenty of training and study, still carry three lights, attach lines to the entrance to find their way back, and carry extra air tanks. Cavers utilize the rule of thirds—use a third of your air to enter, a third to exit on, and a third for emergencies. Cave divers have their own agencies that conduct training and issue certification. Certi-fied cave divers have an excellent safety record, but there is no room for error inside a cave. Caves have claimed the lives of many divers untrained in cave diving, even open water instructors! Cave diving? It's best left to the professionals or those trained amateurs with years of experience.

Treasure Diving

Treasure diving gets a lot of attention. You see pictures in magazines of weathered and waterlogged divers bringing up gold coins and rusted cannon. What a rush! What you don't see is all those same guys coming up with nothing. And they've come up with nothing a whole lot more than they did with gold coins.

Treasure divers spend maybe more time raising money for the search than doing the dives, because this sort of business costs plenty—millions in many cases.

The team spends months or years researching potential treasure sites, hires the most advanced research ships they can afford, then travels thousands of miles to dive waters that are often cold and murky day after day for weeks or months. Seems like a waste of time and trouble, doesn't it?

But, don't tell that to the diver who scored those gold coins or that 16th Century cannon.

There are also laws that govern the treasure diver. No matter how much money you spent or how hard and long you worked, some governments of the world claim that whatever you find in their waters belongs to them.

There are those times, too, when after all the planning, all the money, and all the labor, you locate that Spanish strongbox—only to find that it's empty!

Still, there are cases like the *Atocha*, a Spanish galleon that yielded $20-40,000,000 in treasure—that kind of story keeps treasure divers diving.

Search and Recovery

Search and recovery diving is something else again. Not particularly dangerous under most conditions, this sort of diving is often directed toward finding bodies for the police and locating valuable property that's fallen into the water. The water you're slugging through may be cold or muddy. You might be only ten feet down, but for all the difference it makes, you could be a mile below, since you can't see a thing, and search by feeling your way around.

You might be using special search patterns underwater so as not to miss a single patch of sand or muddy bottom. You might be utilizing a huge "balloon" that you fill with air from your regulator to lift an item to the surface. And you might be doing all this at three o'clock in the morning if that's what's necessary. But finding and recovering is as satisfying as its gets.

Repair and Construction

There are lots of underwater repair jobs, such as welding a busted pipe, reattaching broken wires, beefing up a defective pier, fixing a damaged boat hull, or replacing a rotting gate hinge.

And there's lots of underwater construction, too. Pilings need to be sunken into the ocean floor, and walls need to be erected. There are foundations for buildings and feet for docks, pipes to be laid and seams to be sealed.

Specialty diving is special. Some types provide their own hazards, but also their own unique rewards.

Scuba diving promises worlds of its own—
exploring shipwrecks, getting fascinated by the
equipment, or just cruising the reef looking for
marine life. The thrill of discovery awaits whether
it's diving on a newly discovered wreck or adding
a new species to your personal list of marine life.

CAREERS

By now it's obvious how much fun you can have scuba diving. The question many people ask though, is "Can I make a living at it?"

Sure. But you're not likely to get rich, though diver/writer Peter Benchley made more than a few bucks off his *Jaws* books and movies. Most people in the diving world manage to scratch out a modest income. But ask any of them if they'd trade what they're doing for bigger paychecks, and you'll get the same answer: No way!

Let's list some of the careers people have come up with in this fascinating world of scuba diving:

Divemaster
Instructor
Technician/repairman
Sales representative
Dive shop owner/employee
Photographer/model
Writer
Publisher
Boat captain
Equipment manufacturer
Medic/doctor
Hyperbaric chamber operator
Publicist
Software designer
Treasure hunter
Researcher
Naturalist/ecologist
Travel agent
Artist/illustrator
Filmmaker/videographer
Resort operator
Photo/camera technician
Commercial diver
Military diver

There are also various other careers within each of these listings. Jobs may take you to many parts of the world, or let you stay right in your own neighborhood if you'd prefer.

But, these jobs seldom fall into your lap by accident. Maybe luck plays a role, but luck is usually a matter of preparation meeting opportunity. You hear about an opening at a dive shop, but if you aren't already a diver or an instructor, it may not matter; you wander into a dive resort just after a sales clerk has quit, but if you haven't had some retail experience, you probably won't get the job. Your group's photographer just flooded his camera, but if you don't have one and know how to use it, you just blew a great chance. But with proper training and experience, there are plenty of job openings in the diving world.

SOME FINAL THOUGHTS

You see plenty of divers wearing gloves. They do when they're dealing with hazardous materials or animals, other times it's because of the cold. Sometimes though, it's for neither of those. It's just a habit, or they think they're supposed to be wearing them.

Many dive destinations of the world, particularly in warmer locales, are asking divers to leave their gloves home. Why? Because gloves make it easier to needlessly touch things, such as living coral that took many years to grow just one inch.

The point here is that more divers and leaders in the dive community have come to realize the damage that can be done, even by divers with the best intentions. There are people who'd never in a mil-

There is never a need to touch, harrass or frighten. Simply looking in wonder is joy enough. Even veteran divers look forward to seeing something new on almost every dive.

lion years hassle a bird in its nest, but who'd not give a second thought to tormenting an underwater eel out of its hole with a stick just to take a picture. And folks who go out of their way to avoid treading on a beautiful flower, hit the water and think nothing of grabbing onto a living soft coral branch to steady themselves. Still others who wouldn't ever crush a ground squirrel's hole, don't give a second thought to tossing their boat anchor onto whatever happens to be down there.

The dive flag, besides warning boaters that divers are underwater, is the universal symbol for the diving fraternity. You'll see it on T-shirts, decals, bumper stickers, coffee mugs, dive shop signs, hats and lots of other places.

If we're going to continue to enjoy life underwater and bring our children and grandchildren to it for the same reason, we must protect it. The underwater environment is even more fragile than that above the surface. The animals below are often very delicate, and the slightest upset in their surroundings can be devastating.

Spear fishing is a controversial topic among divers. Some people feel that's why fish were put here, to provide us food; others say a trained diver with a powerful spear gun is no match for a simple fish just swimming around.

A case can be made for spearing for food, I suppose, but there's no argument at all when it comes to spearing for sport. Killing for the sake of killing doesn't belong anywhere.

In much of the world, spear fishing is prohibited if the hunter is using scuba. At least that evens the odds a little by making spear fishermen be free divers.

Some years ago, at a Caribbean island, there was gorgeous six-foot-long green moray eel that lived in a coral clump. Divers had fed it by hand for ages, and when-ever divemasters brought their guests around, the eel came out for the usual snack. One day, a spear fisherman was down there, illegally hunting with scuba gear. He'd never been to this location before, and when the virtually tame eel emerged, expecting its usual taste of squid, the diver freaked and fired. He surely thought he'd saved himself or his buddy from being attacked by this wild moray. Instead, all he did was kill a harmless creature looking for a treat. You've got to use your head more than you use your spear, if spear you must.

Dive safety is everyone's responsibility. Good divers are safe divers. They don't take chances that might endanger themselves, or that might jeopardize those who have come to their rescue.

And they don't dive with equipment that hasn't been looked at in years. Good divers take care of the stuff that'll take care of them.

They don't push their times, their depths or their luck. As we mentioned, the responsible diver plans the dive, then dives the plan.

Scuba diving is one of life's real treats. If you've never tried it but you love the water, contact a nearby dive shop and ask to take lessons. In less than a week, you'll be in the water, breathing effortlessly, experiencing much that the underwater world has to offer. You'll feel weightless and relaxed, peaceful and calm. And you'll see things you never knew existed.

You'll be a diver. Welcome.

The dive boat heads anxiously out to sea for an adventurous day of diving the spectacular reefs and walls of Grand Cayman.

U.S. Training Agencies

**Handicapped Scuba Association
International (HAS)**
1104 El Prado
San Clemente, CA 92672-4637
Phone: (949) 498-4540; Fax: (949) 498-6128
URL: www.hsascuba.com

**International Diving Educators
Association (IDEA)**
PO Box 8427
Jacksonville, FL 32239-8427
Phone: (904) 744-5554; Fax: (904) 743-5425
URL: www.idea-scubadiving.com

**National Academy of Scuba Educators
(NASE)**
1728 Kingsley Avenue, Suite 105
Orange Park, FL 32073
Phone: (800) 728-26273; Fax: (904) 269-2283
URL: www.inet.co.th/cyberclub/hgay/
nase.html

**National Association of Underwater
Instructors (NAUI)**
PO Box 14650
Montclair, CA 91763-1150
Phone: (800) 553-6284; Fax: (909) 621-6405
URL: www.naui.org

**Professional Association of Diving
Instructors (PADI)**
1251 East Dyer Road, Suite 100
Santa Ana, CA 92706-5605
Phone: (800) 729-7234; Fax: (714) 540-2609
URL: www.padi.com

**Professional Diving Instructors
Corporation (PDIC)**
PO Box 3633
Scranton, PA 18505
Phone: (570) 342-1480; Fax: (570) 342-6030
URL: www.pdic-intl.com

Scuba Diving International
18 Elm Street
Topsham, ME 04086
Phone: (888) 778-9073; Fax: (207) 729-4453
URL: www.tdisdi.com

Scuba Schools International (SSI)
2619 Canton Court
Fort Collins, CO 80525-4498
Phone: (800) 892-2702; Fax: (970) 4802-6157
URL: www.ssiusa.com

YMCA Scuba
101 N Wacker Drive
Chicago, IL 60606
Phone: (800) 872-9622; Fax: (312) 977-0894
URL: www.ymcascuba.org